Mixing and Separating

Chris Oxlade

WAYLAND

First published in Great Britain in 2006 by Wayland,
an imprint of Hachette Children's Books

Hachette Children's Books
338 Euston Road, London NW1 3BH

Editor: Hayley Leach
Senior Design Manager: Rosamund Saunders
Designer: Ben Ruocco
Photographer: Philip Wilkins

British Library Cataloguing in Publication Data
Oxlade, Chris
   Mixing and separating. - (Working with materials)
   1.Mixing - Juvenile literature 2.Separation (technology) -
   Juvenile literature
   I.Title 660.2'842

ISBN-10: 0-7502-4905-6
ISBN-13: 978-0-7502-4905-8

Cover photograph: two cooks make a cake mixture.
Photo credits: Jurgen Vogt/Getty Images 8; BSIP/photolibrary 10;
Mike Powell/Getty Images 11; Dave King/Dorling Kindersley 12;
Simon Fraser/Science Photo Library 13; Roger Spooner/Getty
Images 14; Chris Windsor/Getty Images 15; Philip Wilkins 16;
Adam Woolfit/Corbis 17; Roger Stowell/Getty Images 18;
IPS Photo Index/photolibrary 19; Reza Estakhrian/Getty Images 20;
Ryan McVay/Getty Images 21; Douglas Peebles/Corbis 22;
Bojan Brecelj/Corbis 23; Johner/Getty Images cover and 24;
Mediscan/Alamy 25; Philip Wilkins 26-27.

The publishers would like to thank models Philippa and Sophie
Campbell for appearing in the photographs.

CONTENTS

What is a mixture?   6

Mixtures around us   8

Mixing solutions   10

Separating materials   12

Sieving materials   14

Settling and skimming   16

Filtering liquids   18

Filtering gases   20

Evaporation   22

Making new materials   24

Activities   26

Glossary   28

Further information   29

Index   30

Words in **bold** can be found in the glossary on page 28

What is a mixture?

Everything around you is made up of materials. Everyday materials include plastic, metal, water and wood. A mixture is made up of two or more different materials.

↓ *This is a mixture of nuts and raisins.*

Materials are made up of pieces. The pieces can be lumps of materials, or tiny **particles** too small to see. In a mixture, the pieces of different materials are not attached to each other. We can separate them.

↑ *Pouring this mixture through a **colander** separates the pasta from the water.*

Mixtures around us

Many **natural materials** can be mixtures. Milk is a mixture of water, fat, sugar and other materials. Sea water is a mixture of water and materials called salts.

↓ *The smoke from a fire is a mixture. It is made up of hot gases and tiny bits of* **soot**.

← *We can make new colours by mixing together two colours of paint.*

It's a Fact!

The air around us is a mixture of gases. One of the gases is called **oxygen**. It is the gas that we breathe to stay alive.

We can make many different mixtures ourselves. We can mix ingredients together to make tasty foods, such as fruit salad, which is a mixture of different fruits and juice.

Mixing solutions

When you put sugar into tea the sugar slowly disappears. The same thing happens when you put salt into a pan of water for cooking vegetables. The sugar and salt are still there. They are mixed with the water.

↓ *The **granules** of this sugar cube will gradually get smaller until they are too small to see.*

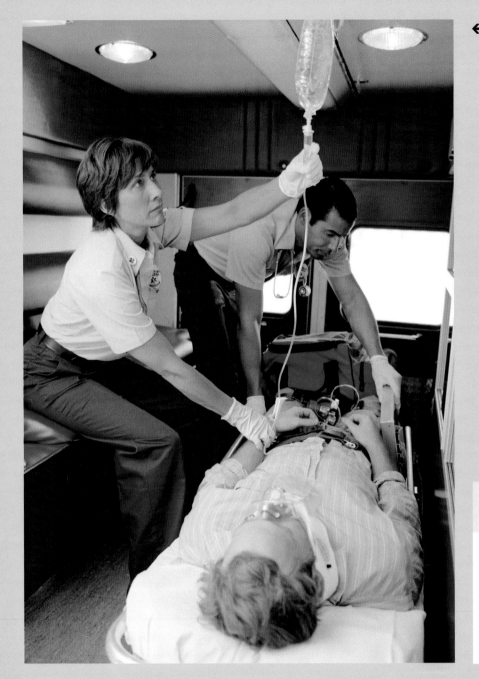

← *Solutions are used in medicine. This patient is being given a salt solution.*

It's a Fact!

Fizzy drinks are a mixture of drink and gas. The gas makes bubbles when you open the can or bottle.

When sugar and salt are mixed in water we say that they **dissolve**. The small pieces of sugar and salt break into tiny particles. This sort of mixture is called a solution.

Separating materials

Sometimes we want to get certain materials from a mixture. Then we have to separate the mixture. For example, we separate peas and cooking water to get the peas.

← *This spoon is full of small holes. It is used to separate beans from cooking water.*

↑ *This giant magnet is picking out a metal called steel.*

We use the **properties** of a material to separate it from a mixture. Properties tell us what a material is like. A property of steel is that it is **magnetic**. We can use a magnet to pull steel paper clips from a mixture of steel and plastic paper clips.

It's a Fact!

Tiny bits of gold are often found in the mud at the bottom of rivers. You can separate the gold from the mud by swirling the mud around in a pan.

Sieving materials

Some mixtures are made up of pieces of solid materials. We can separate the large pieces from the small ones by sieving. A sieve is like a tray with hundreds of holes in the bottom. When the mixture is poured in only small pieces fall through.

↓ *The tiny bits of soil fall through this sieve. The potatoes are left.*

14

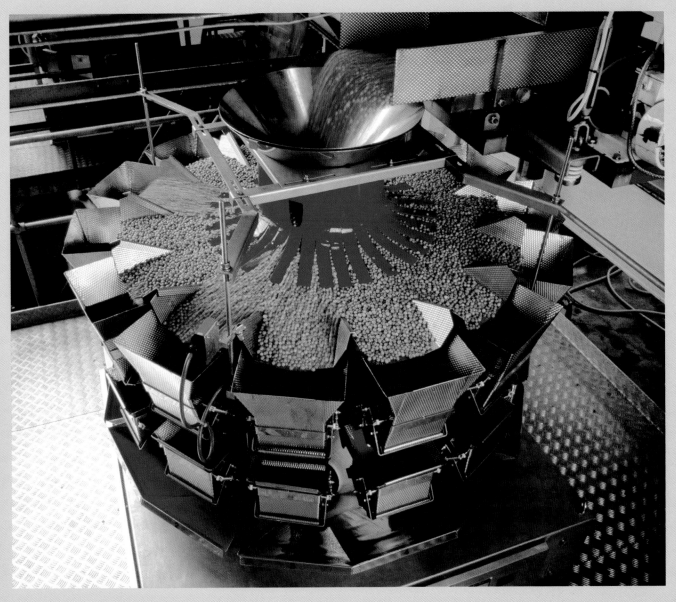

A mixture can be made up of different sized pieces of the same material. We use sieves to separate the mixture of pieces into their different sizes. For example, potatoes from a field can be sorted into large and small sizes using sieves.

↑ *This is a pea-sorting machine. It is sorting the peas into different sizes.*

Settling and skimming

Some mixtures are made up of two liquids mixed together. Others are made up of a liquid and solid pieces mixed together. If we leave mixtures like these standing still they sometimes separate by themselves. We say that the mixture settles.

← If we leave muddy water standing the dirt settles to the bottom.

← *This container of milk will settle to make **curds** and **whey**. The curds will be used to make cheese.*

It's a Fact!

All the dirty water from your toilet, sink and shower goes to a sewage works. It settles in tanks and the clean water is pumped out.

When we let a mixture settle, some materials come up to the top of the mixture. They make a **scum** on the top. We can scoop the scum off. This is called skimming.

Filtering liquids

Some mixtures are made up of bits of solid in a liquid. We can separate the solid and the liquid by filtering. A filter has holes that let liquid through but trap the solid. When we drain vegetables through a colander we are filtering out the water.

← The holes in this filter are too small for the grains of rice to get through.

← *A paper coffee filter lets water and some of the coffee through but traps the larger coffee particles.*

It's a Fact!

Campers sometimes have to drink water from streams. They use a water filter to separate dirt and tiny bugs from the water.

Filters are often made of paper or fabric. These materials are made of thin fibres. There are tiny holes between the fibres. When a mixture is poured onto filter paper, the water seeps through but the solid is trapped.

Filtering gases

Air is a gas that contains dust and other particles. For example, smoke from a fire is a mixture of air and tiny bits of ash. We use air filters to separate the air and the bits of solid. This cleans the air.

↓ *This man's face mask lets air through but stops him breathing in tiny bits of the harmful material.*

← *The paper filter in this vacuum cleaner traps dusty air. The dust collects in a bag which can be thrown away.*

It's a Fact!

Engines need air to work. They suck air in through a filter. This stops dirt getting into the engine.

A vacuum cleaner sucks up a mixture of air and dust. Inside the machine the dust is separated from the air. Filters trap the dust but let the air through. The clean air is blown out again. The dust is stored in the machine.

Evaporation

When the ground dries after rain, the water turns to **water vapour** and mixes with the air. This change is called evaporation. We can use evaporation to separate the parts of a solution.

↓ Salty water is being separated. The water is evaporating, leaving the salt behind.

↑ At this factory, salty water is being distilled to make fresh water.

Sometimes we want to keep the liquid from a solution. We do this using a process called distillation. Liquid evaporates from a solution to make gas. The gas is cooled down and turns back to a liquid.

It's a Fact!

In some countries people use water from the sea for drinking and washing. The salt is separated from the sea water by distillation.

23

Making new materials

Sometimes when we mix materials together we can't separate them again. This is because the materials change when they are mixed with each other. For example, we mix flour, water and other ingredients to make dough for bread.

← *To make a cake you mix flour, eggs, sugar and butter and bake the mixture in an oven.*

24

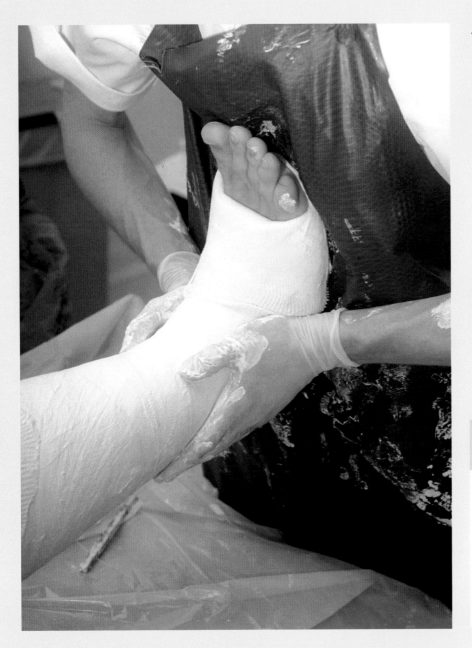

← In hospitals, plaster of Paris is used to make casts for broken limbs.

It's a Fact!

Concrete is made by mixing cement, water, sand and gravel. After the ingredients are mixed, the concrete turns into a solid.

Some materials change when we mix them with water. Plaster of Paris powder turns to thick paste and then goes hard when it is mixed with water. The two materials have changed. We can never get them back.

25

Activities

Separating with magnets

Try this experiment to see how the properties of a material can help to separate a mixture.

What you need

steel paper clips	plastic bowl
rice	magnet

① Put some paper clips and some rice into a plastic bowl and mix them together.

② Now slowly move the magnet through the mixture. The paper clips stick to the magnet. This separates them from the rice.

③ You can also try this experiment using other materials, such as nails and flour or hairgrips and buttons.

Settling muddy water

Find out how mud can be separated from water.

What you need	
jar	old spoon
water	earth from the garden

① Fill the jar with water.

② Add a spoonful of earth to the jar and stir. The muddy water is a mixture of water and earth. Always wash your hands after touching soil.

③ Put the jar on a shelf and leave it. Look every hour to see what has happened.

④ The mixture soon begins to settle. Bits of rock sink to the bottom. Rotting bits of plants float to the top. After a few hours the water becomes clear again.

Glossary

colander a bowl-shaped container with small holes in the bottom

concrete a material used in building that goes very hard when it sets

curds a solid material made when milk is separated

dissolve to break up into tiny pieces in a liquid

granules small pieces of a material, one or two millimetres across

magnetic a material that is pulled towards a magnet

natural material any material that comes from the ground, plants or animals, such as rock or wood

oxygen a gas found in the air. We need oxygen to breathe

particle a very small piece of material, too small for you to see

property tells us what a material is like

scum a layer of solid material floating on top of a liquid

soot tiny, black particles of burned material

water vapour water in the form of a gas

whey a watery material made when milk is separated

Further information

BOOKS

How We Use: Metals/Paper/Rubber/Wood
by Chris Oxlade, Raintree (2005)

A Material World: It's Glass/It's Metal/It's Plastic/It's Wood
by Kay Davies and Wendy Oldfield, Wayland (2006)

Investigating Science: How do we use materials?
by Jacqui Bailey, Franklin Watts (2005)

WEBSITES

www.bbc.co.uk/schools/revisewise/science/materials/09_act.shtml
Animated examples and a quiz about changing materials

www.chem4kids.com/files/matter_intro.html
All about materials, including mixtures and solutions

PLACES TO VISIT

Eureka, Halifax
www.eureka.org.uk

Glasgow Science Centre
www.glasgowsciencecentre.org

The Science Museum, London
www.sciencemuseum.org.uk

Index

All the numbers in **bold** refer to photographs.

bread 24

cake 24, **24**
coffee 19, **19**
colander 7, **7**, 18
concrete 25

distillation 23, **23**

engines 21
evaporation 22, **22**-23

face mask 20, **20**
filtering 18-19, **18-19**
fire 8, **8**, 20
fruit 9

gas 8, **8**, 9, 11, 20-21, 23
gold 13

magnet 13, **13**, 26, **26**
metal 6, 13, **13**
milk 8, 17, **17**
natural material 8

nuts and raisins 6, **6**

oxygen 9

paint 9, **9**
particles 7, 11
pasta 7, **7**
plaster of Paris 25, **25**
potatoes 14, **14**, 15

salt 10, 11, **11**, 22, **22**, 23
sea water 8
settling 16, **16**, 27, **27**
sewage 17
sieving 14, **14**-15, 18, **18**
skimming 17, **17**
smoke 8, **8**
solutions 10-11, 22-23
spoon 12, **12**
steel 13, **13**
sugar 10, **10**, 11

vacuum cleaner 21, **21**

water 7, **7**, 12, **12**, 16, **16**, 18, **18**, 19, **19**, 22, **22**, 23, **23**, 27, **27**